MEDICS IN THE MOUNTAINS

The Story of
Edgar and Elizabeth Miller

by
ELEANOR PRESTON CLARKSON

Sincerely yours

Edgar and Elizabeth

Friendship Press New York

Jul/72

CONTENTS

CHAPTER ONE
The Reunion

"What a pleasant surprise," said Elizabeth Miller, M.D., to herself as she read the letter she had just opened. "It's years since I've seen Bethel—almost thirty years since we attended medical school together." She read the letter again. Memories, some happy, and some sad, seemed to drift between the lines; her glasses fogged over.

"Edgar," she said that night at dinner, "you'll never guess who's coming to see us."

Dr. Edgar Miller looked across the table at his wife and thought of possibilities—one of his former patients, one of her former patients, a past member of their Bible class at Richardson Park Methodist Church, one of the Chinese couples who enjoyed meeting informally in the Millers' spacious kitchen and cooking delicious exotic meals. Perhaps son Edgar, Jr. ("Tyke") and his wife Jane or daughter Elizabeth ("Biddy") and her husband Bill had prepared a surprise. There were so many possibilities that he decided it was useless to try to guess.

He smiled. "I can't imagine," he said. "Who?"

"Bethel and Robert Fleming."

"No! Why, I didn't know they were coming east. Their furlough is over, isn't it?"

"It would have been, but their son Bob hasn't completely recovered from the lung surgery he had last year. Their leave has been extended. Bethel says they are initiating a medical mission in Nepal; they've been raising money for it. We'll have to give them a good rest—they must be exhausted."

Thus the Flemings, longtime missionaries in India, journeyed east from their home in Albion, Michigan, to visit the Doctors Miller in Wilmington, Delaware. The year was 1955. Weariness gradually dropped from them as they savored the warmth and generosity of the Millers' hospitality and their genuine interest in hearing about the strange and wonderful way that they had been invited to Nepal after the many years they had spent in India.

"On the wings of a bird," Bethel said, "truly on the wings of many birds."

"Rudyard Kipling had something to do with it, too,"

said Robert. "Remember how he wrote in 'The Explorer':

> Something hidden. Go and find it.
> Go and look behind the Ranges—
> Something lost behind the Ranges.
> Lost and waiting for you. Go!

"For twenty-five years we watched the Himalayas from our station in Mussoorie and dreamed of something waiting for us behind the ranges. Then Bishop Pickett read a new appointment for us at the Delhi Conference in October, 1953: we were to assume the responsibilities of superintendent of the medical mission to Nepal. Sometimes it seems as if we might wake up and find it isn't true—still a dream."

"You know of course about Robert's lifelong interest in ornithology," said Bethel, "and of his association with the Chicago Museum of Natural History, because he's published articles and written letters about it from time to time. However, we never thought so much would happen after he and Dr. Carl Taylor, medical missionary, and three others were permitted to enter Nepal for a three-months' scientific expedition in 1949. The museum underwrote the cost of that; it was a great success for them and for us."

"We trekked four or five hundred miles through

some of the most wonderful country in the world," Robert said, "and we collected species of birds never seen before. Nepal is a land where few Americans have ever gone. Sometimes we visited areas no American had ever seen.

"Word about Dr. Taylor ran ahead of us along many of the trails; he was overwhelmed by people seeking medical attention. I remember thinking at one time that it must have been very much like this when Christ healed the sick and the multitude walked miles to be with him.

"At Pokhara in West Nepal Dr. Taylor performed twenty-one major operations right out under the blue sky. Then he had to stop because his gloves became unusable."

"When Robert went back in 1951—in December—I went with him," said Bethel. "It was quite an experience. Would you believe it? I traveled part of the way in a *dandy*."

"A *dandy*! What's that?" asked Elizabeth.

"It's a kind of chair, woven of cane, but instead of having legs, it is fastened like a litter to two poles. Four men are needed to carry it on their shoulders. Now I'm glad to say they have begun airplane service into Kathmandu."

"Between my two visits," Robert continued, "a revolution took place in Nepal. For a hundred years the Rana family had been hereditary prime ministers. They were so powerful that they could exile a king or hold him prisoner in his own palace, though few subjects realized this. The last of the prime ministers, the one in power when I made my first expedition, had sixteen sons and sixteen daughters. He built a palace for each of the sons. He was overthrown in 1951. Now that the political situation has changed, some of the palaces may be rented."

"In fact, we've been offered one called Shanta Bhawan for our new hospital," interrupted Bethel, "but we need to find a sponsor to underwrite the cost of the rent."

"You're getting ahead of the story. We'd better tell about the way we began," said Robert.

They related how they had asked the Nepalese Government to allow them to establish a Christian mission of healing in this land where it was so desperately needed.

The Ministry of Health, though still reluctant to admit foreigners, had been so impressed with the medical service given by the missionaries during the scientific expeditions that it finally agreed to allow the Christian missionaries a period of five years in which to work. Permission was granted to start a hospital in Tansen,

West Nepal, and maternity and child welfare centers in the valley of Kathmandu. The missionaries must train Nepalese workers, must pay the costs involved in their work.

On January 7, 1954, Bethel opened the first clinic with twenty patients at the valley town of Bhatgaon, eight miles from Kathmandu. Seven weeks later two hundred patients came.

In Kathmandu the government made available an old cholera hospital, and the first five workers under the newly constituted United Medical Mission to Nepal— one Indian, one Canadian and three from the United States—representing three different denominations—set about with a will to make it usable. Dr. Bob became superintendent for the Kathmandu area, to attend to all but medical details. The staff wielded blowtorches, used quantities of sandpaper, disinfectant, whitewash, paint and window glass and in one month of hard work prepared it for the opening day, February 20, 1954. Some eighty or ninety guests gathered for the ceremony at which the prime minister, Mr. M. P. Koirala, made the principal address and cut the ribbon.

"The house we leased to live in," said Robert, "had one bed, two chairs, no bathrooms, no water connections, no screening, but we made it do.

"Nepal is a remote place, no question about that, and the living conditions are primitive everywhere. Travel is difficult and most of the time on foot on precarious trails. The telephone system was the private plaything of the Ranas but now the government is trying to extend it. The water is bad because the people know little about sanitation or preventive medicine."

"The diseases are different from those you treat here," commented Bethel. "Leprosy, filariasis, cholera, typhoid. Tuberculosis is perhaps the worst scourge. Thousands have malaria."

"The Constitution says we can't convert others to our religion," said Robert, "but we can worship together and we do. On Easter in 1954 just before we came home, over thirty Christians and one Nepalese Hindu gathered on a housetop for a dawn service. We represented Nepal, India, Switzerland, Britain, Canada and the United States. One man sang, a Catholic father prayed, a woman read the Scriptures, and as we listened again to the Easter story, the sun rose out of the Himalayas. God seemed very close to us all."

The little group of friends exchanged wonderful talk about hopes and dreams and challenges and rewards. Finally, Bethel said, "We need doctors almost more than we need financial support if the mission is to succeed." She paused, looked thoughtfully across at

11

Elizabeth and asked, "Why don't you two come back with us?"

Elizabeth turned to Edgar. "Why don't we?" she said simply.

Edgar answered, "I don't know any reason why not. The children are grown up and happily married. We can turn our practice over to younger doctors, sell the house and go."

They applied to a somewhat bewildered Board of Missions.

"Here are two people in their late fifties who have always wanted to be missionaries—this time they wish to go to Nepal. They're both doctors and we need doctors—but still—will their health stand the climate and the living conditions? Do these people have any idea what they're getting into? They'll find that living in the Himalayas is a lot different from living in Wilmington, Delaware."

The Millers explained that this represented no sudden decision on their part. Years ago, before they were married, they had applied to the Board of Missions for missionary service but had been rejected because they were five thousand dollars in debt for their education and could not possibly liquidate such an amount on missionaries' salaries.

In fact, their commitment dated back even further.

An Indian woman, dressed in a colorful sari, had spoken to Elizabeth's high school class in Williamsport, Pennsylvania, and at the end of her talk, pointed to Elizabeth and two others and said, "I want you and you and you to become doctors and come to India. India needs you." Elizabeth had decided at that time to be a mission doctor in India, an aim encouraged by her parents.

Edgar had started to study for the ministry. When a Student Volunteer speaker came to Dickinson College and spoke to a group of young men about the need for foreign missionaries, Edgar promised to be a foreign missionary. Shortly after this he switched to pre-medical courses. He dreamed of serving in China but was willing to accept assignment to India. Meanwhile, to stay in college he worked a full shift every night as a telegraph operator.

Elizabeth was born in Oldwich, New Jersey, Edgar in New Freedom, Pennsylvania. They met at Dickinson College when he was a senior and she a freshman, and attended Student Volunteer gatherings together. Their interest in each other grew even after they separated to go to different medical schools. Edgar attended the medical school of the University of Maryland and Elizabeth studied at the Woman's Medical College of Pennsylvania.

They explained their background to the Board of Missions in 1955. It took them several months to answer all the questions, fill out all the blanks, assemble and crate all the equipment needed, arrange all the necessary clearance, provide for their respective practices and in addition dispose of their cars and their house.

Meeting the personnel committee of the Board of Missions represented the final hurdle to acceptance. One member of the committee, Mrs. John Pearson, recalled the interview vividly.

"That wonderful couple," she said. "We were delighted to accept them. We always asked if the candidates had any questions and Edgar did. He had quantities of expensive medical equipment he proposed to take with him but he was afraid it might not be possible because the rules say there's a strict limit on the amount of baggage the board will pay to transport. We made an exception in a hurry, I can tell you."

So more than thirty-five years after an Indian woman doctor had challenged Elizabeth and the Student Volunteer leader had inspired Edgar, the Millers were commissioned by Bishop Arthur J. Moore at Buck Hill Falls, Pennsylvania, on January 20, 1956, and began the long-awaited adventure.

After the ceremony, the new missionaries gathered

14

in the reception room to receive the greetings of friends, relatives and well-wishers. As these poured out of the assembly hall and approached the reception room, the first of them saw Elizabeth throw her arms around her husband and heard her say, "Oh Edgar, we're missionaries at last!"

CHAPTER TWO
The Journey

When the Isthmian Line freighter, *Steel Surveyor*, weighed anchor from her dock in Brooklyn, New York, late on the evening of February 8, 1956, she had Robert and Bethel Fleming, their daughter Sally Beth, and Edgar and Elizabeth Miller as passengers.

In addition to her cargo, she carried 101 crates, boxes and packages belonging to the Millers. At the head of the list came the ambulance and the jeep they had bought with the proceeds of the sale of their two cars, the X-ray machine donated by the Richardson Park Methodist Church, an electrocardiograph from the Philipsburg, Pennsylvania, Methodist Church, a set of surgical instruments furnished by the West Presbyterian Church of Wilmington, and the Millers' complete medical library supplemented by the Wilmington Academy of Medicine for an estimated total of two tons of books. Toward the cost of other equipment and supplies, they had received substantial gifts of cash from grateful patients, a Roman Catholic priest, and their milkman.

"Take some of your nice things," a seasoned missionary wife advised Elizabeth. "They'll give you a lift when you need it." So Elizabeth had carefully packed her blue Wedgwood plates and teacups. More than one Westerner, stopping for a meal at the Millers' home in Kathmandu, exclaimed with incredulous delight on seeing these, "Wedgwood? Here? How nice!" Thus, they gave others a lift too.

The Flemings also had a ton or so of supplies. Transforming a palace into a hospital takes a lot of equipment.

"Our journey began with a mixture of sadness and joy," Edgar remarked later, "and it lasted fifty days." They were sad about leaving Tyke and Jane, Biddy, Bill and little Tyrie Lee, just born, about leaving Elizabeth's father, the Reverend J. E. A. Bucke, and a host of friends. Anticipation of all that lay ahead welled up in them. They were glad to be going out as medical missionaries, on their way to Nepal, the "hermit kingdom," as Robert Fleming so often called it.

Indeed it seemed providential that a people more than ten thousand miles from the United States chose this moment in history to break out of a hundred years of isolation and invite doctors from the West at the very time circumstances made the Flemings and Millers available.

The *Steel Surveyor* rolled and pitched across the wintry Atlantic and through the Mediterranean to Beirut, Lebanon, 5,300 miles without a stop. The Millers and the Flemings relaxed and rested. The months of preparation had been unusually taxing for both couples. The visits to sponsoring churches, shopping for so much hospital equipment and supplies and the personal needs for five years, the packing, the immunization shots—all the necessary adjuncts to a missionary's life—were behind them. They had ample time to contemplate the future and discuss plans.

"I know Kathmandu has changed," said Robert. "After we left on furlough, King Tribhuvan went to Switzerland for treatment but died there of a heart attack. Crown Prince Mahendra has become king. We met him personally when he and his two brothers called on us in February, 1953, to examine our bird collection."

"We always get back to birds sooner or later," Bethel remarked. "Did we tell you that the Chicago Museum of Natural History has made Bob an honorary field associate in zoology and has also named him a contributor for having sent them speciments valued at over $1,000?"

She continued, "All the recent reports from Nepal about the United Medical Mission indicate that the work is growing rapidly. More people are coming to the dispensaries than can be cared for. Kathmandu hospital has a waiting list for those seeking admission. Since we left, Dr. Carl Friedericks has opened a permanent hospital in Tansen, West Nepal, but he desperately needs more staff."

"I hope the new road from India to Nepal is passable again," said Robert. "Shortly after it opened to the public in August, 1954, it was blocked by a hundred landslides.

"We understand King Mahendra and the Nepalese officials are promoting tourism. The first tourists seemed enthusiastic about their visit to Kathmandu. This can change many things."

From Beirut to Alexandria to Karachi to Bombay, the *Steel Surveyor* plowed steadily on her way, stopping at Colombo, Ceylon, before proceeding north to Visakhapatnam and on through the Bay of Bengal. By the time she took on the pilot to steer her eighty miles up the shifting, treacherous Hooghly River to Calcutta, Robert Fleming said he was ready to get off and run.

After landing at Calcutta on March 28, the Flemings

and the Millers struggled for two and one half weeks to clear their effects through customs. Prickly heat in humid subtropical temperatures that ranged from 104 to 112 degrees spoiled any thrill they felt over being in one of the world's busiest ports, capital city of India until 1912. From the docks to the customs house then back to the docks they went in a fruitless round day after day.

On April 15, they agreed that the Millers, Dr. Bethel and Sally Beth would go to Kathmandu by plane and Robert would stay behind to deal with the customs problems alone.

Sometimes over the mountains, sometimes between them, the little plane flew. As it passed between the peaks, it flew so close it seemed in danger of scraping the farmers from their fields on the terraced slopes. Then the broad valley of Kathmandu came into view, emerald green with growing wheat, and the plane landed on the single airstrip. It taxied to a stop by the mud shack with a thatched roof that served as the Kathmandu airport. Thus did the Millers arrive in Nepal.

Of his own journey, Robert wrote later:

"After the 28th day, with almost everything still in customs, a driver and I jumped into the new jeep and started for Kathmandu. We drove all night on the Grand Trunk Road to our Methodist Ushagram Colony, caught a wink of sleep and were off again toward Patna. It took us half a day to cross the Ganges River in a country boat. Beyond, the road was terrible. We covered the 700 miles in 75 hours and arrived in Kathmandu in the dead of night. We routed out a sleepy guard behind a high wall and asked him where we could find Shanta Bhawan. 'This is it,' he mumbled. When Bethel saw me at 2 A.M. covered with dust, she must have thought I was a ghost. That was journey's end."

CHAPTER THREE
Everything a First

For the Millers it was a case of love at first sight—
the beautiful valley of Kathmandu, the friendly Nepalese, the rare glimpses of the glorious snowcapped peaks
of the Himalayas, hidden by clouds more often than
not at this time of year.

As befits a palace, Shanta Bhawan had marble floors,
wall mirrors, chandeliers in all of its forty rooms—even
in the bathrooms. Electric lights, powered by a generator installed in Kathmandu years before, gave light of
uncertain brilliance. Sometimes one could stare right
into the bulb and observe no more than a glow.

The Flemings and the Millers divided the third floor
between them for living quarters, leaving the first and
second floors for the hospital proper. The Millers found
the arrangements quite different from their comfortable
house in Wilmington, but this did not faze them.

Visitors inspecting Shanta Bhawan remembered Edgar's hearty laugh that started deep within him and bubbled out.

"We have running water," he sometimes explained, "when our runner boys carry it to us. We have central heating when we carry our little kerosene heater to the center of the place where we sit."

Ten wooden beds, a staff of eight—two missionary nurses, two laboratory technicians, three M.D.'s—the Millers and Dr. Bethel—and Robert Fleming as administrator—thus Edgar tabulated the resources of the United Mission Hospital as they began their work together on April 16, 1956, the day after their arrival in Kathmandu.

Kathmandu! An ancient city founded in 723 that received its modern name almost a thousand years later. It derives from two words—Kath Mandir—literally, "the city of the wooden temple," a reference to the temple of Goraknath, which legend said was made entirely from the wood of one tree. Ever since its completion in 1596 it has drawn people to the valley to marvel at such an achievement. Now, the Millers learned, some five or six thousand temples, shrines and pagodas dot the valley —as many shrines as houses, some said.

Through the city they could see the sacred Bagmati River, tributary of the Ganges. Here the Nepalese take those who are dying, for they regard the stream as the portal between life and death. Along its banks burning ghats stood ready for the cremation of the dead.

Buddha was born in Nepal about 2500 years ago, and Buddhist beliefs permeate its culture. Some believe the design of the pagoda originated in Nepal and was later copied in China and Japan. The people have blended Buddhism with Hinduism. Hindu shrines are sacred to Buddhists and statues of Hindu gods stand in Buddhist *stupas*. The people believe that their king is the incarnation of the Hindu god Vishnu.

Hindus from India and Buddhists from Tibet; Gurkha soldiers, the famed fighting men of the British army from the villages of western Nepal; Sherpas from the north, mountain tribesmen renowned throughout the world for their participation in the conquests of Annapurna, Lhotse, Everest; the Newars, noted artisans, carvers of stone and wood, workers in brass and silver and semiprecious stones, long residents of this valley— all jostled each other in the bazaars.

The cries of the vendors, the lowing of beasts, the tinkle of temple bells assailed the ears while the heady fragrance of burning incense and of fresh flowers mingled in the nose with the unmistakable odors rising from open sewers running through the streets. Half-starved, diseased dogs roamed unchecked.

White palaces contrasted with dusty red brick houses with tile roofs and earthen floors. Narrow twisting lanes overhung with intricately carved wooden balconies characterized the old part of the city.

And the broad sweep of the *maidan*, as the parade ground was called, lay ready for use on ceremonial occasions. The Nepalese love pageantry; their calendar is filled with the dates of festivals.

The Millers marveled at the strength of the country people—barefoot for the most part—the soles of their feet as tough as leather. The women bent double under their loads of firewood, their eyes no more than three feet above the ground. They could not possibly see where they were going; yet they found their way. A curious Westerner who persuaded one woman to let him lift her load estimated that it weighed one hundred pounds. Wiry, slender, none of the Nepalese appeared more than five feet tall.

Singha Durbar, former palace of the hereditary prime minister, given over to government offices now, looked remarkably like Versailles. Everything to build it and furnish its hundreds of rooms had been brought in on the backs of porters over the mountain trails from India, over the swaying suspension bridges that crossed the rivers. Incredible. Yet there it stood.

"How natural the Nepalese are," Elizabeth noted.

"Pretense and apologies seem foreign to their nature." She found them gentle, responsive, friendly, patient, hard-working, honest.

And such need! With Dr. Bethel Fleming, the Millers plunged into work in the hospital clinic, trying to stem the tide of human misery, treating sick people who had long been without care of even hope. Diseases they'd never seen before challenged their skills. The pitiful condition of victims of leprosy particularly tore at their heartstrings. They found tuberculosis, intestinal parasites, malnutrition, dysentery, typhoid, diphtheria, rabies. From time to time, dreaded cholera swept through the villages taking a terrible toll. One estimate of the expected life span of the Nepalese put it at twenty-six years.

One patient in these early days presented a heart-breaking series of problems to the staff. For a year he had suffered from a draining wound in his side caused by an intestinal fistula and had been carried ten miles to Shanta Bhawan. Edgar diagnosed the case as tuberculosis and prescribed anti-TB drugs.

After two weeks of this treatment, he found the man and his wife weeping and learned that they had given up all hope. Surgery was clearly indicated but the hospital had no staff surgeon. Occasionally they were able to call upon the USOM (United States Operations Mission) surgeon, but not in extreme cases such as this one.

Edgar suggested that the patient might be referred to the surgeon at the Scottish mission hospital at Raxaul on the Nepal-India border. However, he explained that they would need money for the trip and for what would probably be a prolonged stay at the Raxaul hospital. As he made rounds the next day he discovered a goldsmith cutting jewelry from the wife's ears and fingers. Their total resources added up to 48 rupees (about $7.00).

The journey to Raxaul would involve a 45-minute plane trip to Simra and then a 15-mile trip in a jeep. In addition, it would be necessary to engage a *sati* (companion) for the trip, since the wife and two children could not go.

Just at this time Elizabeth received a hundred dollar gift from someone who left its use entirely to her. She offered this to cover the expenses of the patient and his family. The whole family wept over the father's departure; they never expected to see him again.

Even though it was necessary to operate in two stages and the stay in Raxaul lasted six months, the patient returned completely cured. In addition, he had become a Christian.

He learned to be a hospital technician. In his home village of Bhatgaon he held Bible classes and taught

Sunday school. His Hindu family disowned him; undaunted, his wife became a Christian too. Elizabeth and Edgar thought this was an outstanding example of what Paul meant when he said we are all members of the same body in Christ. They didn't give the money, they didn't perform the surgery, the conversion of the patient took place in another country—yet surely they and the rest of the staff of Shanta Bhawan played a part in it all.

The hospital was always full. When all the beds were occupied, patients cheerfully slept on the floor, on Edgar's examining table, in the halls—anywhere. Their *satis*—friends or relatives who came with them to prepare their food, give them water, attend to their needs —slept on the floor as a matter of course. All insisted that this represented no hardship because they slept on the floor at home.

The Nepalese drink from a jar by holding it far above their heads, tipping its contents into their mouths without touching their lips. This custom made it easy for nurses to administer liquid medicines or water to patients lying on the floor—as one waters the flowers in a garden—otherwise, caring for them presented many problems.

Not only did the three missionary doctors serve the hospital and its village clinics, but they were called upon to attend the royal family and government officials as well as tourists.

The secretary of communications for Nepal, General Surendra, had helped the staff to rent Shanta Bhawan, but their request for telephone service had gone unfilled for ten months. Then the General became one of their first surgery patients. Not only did he recover satisfactorily from his appendectomy, he had the hospital telephone installed as soon as he returned to his office.

Edgar learned early the wisdom of putting his appointment book into his pocket whenever he was invited to a social occasion. Because he was a cardiologist, he had entrée to the royal household at once, for the Queen Mother had a troublesome heart condition.

Thus from the very beginning of their missionary work, the Millers found themselves immersed in Nepalese medical problems from the palace to the humblest thatched village huts in the valley.

They rose at 5:30 A.M., at 6:00 ate breakfast prepared by their faithful houseman, Koncha—oatmeal, fried eggs, toast, powdered coffee. They laughed when they discovered the oatmeal tasted unaccountably of mothballs and ate their entire supply, anyway, trying all sorts of "additives" to mask the flavor.

After breakfast, they shared the morning devotions with others of the United Mission staff, made hospital rounds, conducted the outpatient clinic at the hospital some days, village outpatient clinics on others, joined in consultations with visiting doctors, worked up the day's records, and maintained an extensive correspondence with interested people in the U.S.A. whose financial support was so vital to the mission.

One night a week the whole staff ate a meal together in the hospital dining room—a Nepalese meal of rice, curry and *dal* (lentils), with tea and fruit for dessert. After dinner, they shared a hymn sing. They went to bed by 9:30 or 10:30.

On May 2, 1956 at the precise moment declared to be the most auspicious by the royal astrologers, the coronation of King Mahendra took place on the *maidan*. The staff of Shanta Bhawan attended and sat in especially reserved seats, an indication of the approval and support accorded their efforts by this forward-looking thirty-five-year-old king.

Many hopeful signs gave promise of a new day for Nepal. Traditionally, the king of Nepal always had two wives. King Mahendra had one queen only. He abolished the ancient custom of wet-nurses for his children. He mingled with his people in a way that had never been possible for his father. Because of the repressive measures employed by the Ranas, a broad formal education had been denied this young prince, but he worked diligently to inform himself on many subjects. Each day *The Rising Nepal,* the English language newspaper, carried a brief message to his people from their king urging a united effort to make Nepal prosper.

Those present at the coronation from other lands must surely have wondered whether King Mahendra could possibly overcome the formidable obstacles that lay ahead—a nation 95 percent illiterate, an agricultural economy operating at little more than a subsistence level, and a lack of resources that called for massive programs of foreign aid (both technological and financial) if this small country were to succeed in leaping from a feudal system to a viable modern society. There remained the overriding question: Could Nepal steer a neutral course politically in spite of being bordered on the one hand by democratic India and on the other by Communist China?

His father before him had surmounted tremendous difficulties in freeing his people from a despotic, degrading and corrupt rule and setting up a democratic regime. King Mahendra gave every indication that he intended to pursue his father's enlightened policies for Nepal.

The days slipped into weeks. The spring wheat had been harvested in the valley. The year's second crop—rice—grew in the paddies.

"We have been here twelve weeks now," Edgar wrote, "and our health has been good, although we have each lost ten pounds."

Two-thirds of the equipment they had brought on the *Steel Surveyor,* including the X-ray machine needed so badly, was still tied up in customs in Calcutta in spite of all Robert Fleming or anyone else could do.

Not everyone trusted these doctors from the West. They encountered difficulties with Hindu beliefs, with astrologers who said the time was not auspicious for treatment. Once they were ousted from a place where they had been holding a village clinic because the owner said the gods were angry.

"When I think how our Lord was ridiculed, misunderstood and scorned," Edgar wrote at this time, "what few bumps we have are as nothing."

At the end of September, 1956, Robert Fleming reported: "Our expanding hospital program makes it necessary to provide more staff quarters. Behind Shanta Bhawan is a well-constructed cow shed which we are now converting into a nurses' home. A crew of workmen has knocked windows into walls, replaced miniature doors so one can walk into a room without banging his head, have ripped out sloping floors and have put in plumbing and wiring. All this has cost more than we had anticipated so we have had to hold up the order for furniture and furnishings until our financial position improves.

"Shanta Bhawan, rented for us by the Methodist Church in Barrington, Illinois, looks more like a hospital every day. In the operating room, Rudy Friesen, our young Mennonite maintenance man, has hung the big shadowless lamp, a gift of the First Methodist Church, Kalamazoo, Michigan. Miss Elizabeth Hill is in charge of this operating room; her mission, the Disciples of Christ, has given us several major pieces of equipment including a fine autoclave and gas machine. Mrs. Eunice Stephens has an excellent laboratory on the first floor and is giving technician's training to three Christian Nepalese boys. The old movie hall is now our busy outpatient clinic, complete with office, dispensing and examining rooms. Our Prayer Room is just off the garden and has new benches. The X-ray machine has come. We plan for an official opening and hope the King of Nepal will be our chief speaker."

In October, the Millers had a breathing spell during the Dussera festival, the biggest time of the year in Kathmandu. Patients cleared out of the clinics and wards in order to be home. Schools were closed, all business stopped in the bazaars. Dr. Bethel Fleming spent three weeks in the Mussoorie hill station in North India where Sally Beth attended the Woodstock School.

Elizabeth and Edgar helped celebrate the Methodist centennial in Lucknow. On their way to India they met hundreds of Nepalese streaming back to Kathmandu or to their own villages for the long holiday.

True, they had the X-ray machine, but some of its parts had been damaged in transit. More delays followed while the damaged parts were replaced and a Delhi technician was flown in to install it. Eight months from the time it was unloaded in Calcutta Edgar used it. As the facilities of the hospital improved, so did some of the living arrangements for the staff.

"Some nights are quite warm," Edgar wrote. "On others we need a thin blanket because of the cool breezes. The mosquitoes make their nightly raids and to a light sleeper sound like approaching airplanes. But instead of carrying bombs, they are to a certain extent loaded with malaria or filariasis. However, Dr. Elizabeth had the carpenter erect two handsome shelters in our bedroom which protect us from these deadly night raids. We feel very secure, but our beds look like those of the Louis XIV period."

They treated as many as 150 patients per week in the outpatient department of the hospital, and examined two hundred patients per week in the village clinics.

"We feel inadequate; our equipment is inadequate; but when we think of how you are undergirding us, then we have faith," Elizabeth wrote back to the U. S.

Edgar summed up his feelings at this time: "There is something about this work—either the usual strain and stress, or the weather, or the strain of trying to get the language—that makes one awfully tired. I would attribute it to our age, but upon talking to the young missionaries, I find the same complaint. I can assure you being a missionary is no easy job. However, it has a lot of compensations and thrills."

"Why have you come?" People asked frequently during those first years of Shanta Bhawan Hospital. "Is it to pile up merit with your God?" This seemed a natural question to come from people more familiar with the whirring of Buddhist prayer wheels than with these Christians who were forbidden to evangelize openly by the terms of their agreement. All the staff saw the conditions laid upon their mission as a challenge as they sought to show in their lives and service something of the love of Christ. All drew strength from the very fact of their united mission—interdenominational, international, interracial—the first time a Protestant missionary effort had ever been mounted as the combined enterprise of many boards and agencies, each with its own policies, its own salary scale. Problems arose, of course. However, the group presented a united front, a united Christian front to the world about them.

Both Millers looked deep within themselves at their own Christianity. They found it sobering to think that they were the first Christians many of these people had ever seen.

Everything they did was a first. Setting up a hospital in a palace, conducting clinics in villages no doctor had ever seen before, giving injections, taking X-rays, performing surgery, training the first Nepalese nurses and hospital workers. They felt privileged to pioneer in such an enterprise, and often wished they were thirty years younger.

CHAPTER FOUR
Village Clinics

Village clinic days held special joys for the Millers, though in the beginning they involved slow and difficult travel as well as makeshift working conditions. Originally Elizabeth had planned to study the language as they jolted along, but the roughness of the journey and other factors soon made her abandon the idea.

For one thing the trips afforded the doctors many opportunities to observe the Nepalese going about their daily tasks, living their normal lives, something they never tired of watching.

In one sense the scene shifted constantly with the days and the seasons, and there was always something new. In another sense, what they saw was timeless. People were doing the same things at the same time in the same way as their fathers and grandfathers before them. Generations of patient toilers had scratched an existence from these terraced mountain slopes, these hidden valleys nestling beneath the formidable snowy peaks of the Himalayas.

Men tilled the soil with heavy short-handled hoes, backs bent low to the task. Chop, chop, chop—up to ninety-seven strokes without a pause. Elizabeth counted them. Women followed the men to break up the loosened clods with long-handled wooden mallets. Human harrows, they frequently had their babies strapped on their backs, but even so, were able to pound longer— 263 strokes without stopping—because they stood erect. Elizabeth counted those, too, one day.

Primitive, primitive, so much of it, bending over the fields or straining up mountain trails. Even the use of the wheel had just come to Nepal—centuries after other lands had found it lightened their labor. Road building was done by hand with the simplest sort of tools. People winnowed grain using flat, woven baskets and spread it to dry in the open. They threshed their rice outdoors, too, and hulled it with heavy hand- or foot-operated pounding devices. One could easily imagine he had left the twentieth century behind and was seeing at first hand the life of Bible times, with its threshing floors and village wells.

The Nepalese loved the rain and worked in it happily. Laborers and porters wore strange contrivances on their heads to protect themselves and the burdens on their backs. These afforded effective protection but gave them an odd appearance—like walking chicken coops. They were made of stripped bamboo lined with leaves, and they shed water as effectively as any plastic model from the West.

Drought could be frightening to the farmers, for crop failure meant hunger to many. So real was the threat of famine in 1958 that a royal edict went forth, backed by the priests and astrologers, to the effect that the sacred cows must be led to the Bagmati River and milked into it. To the complete surprise of the Flemings and the Millers and the others of the United Mission—but to no one else—it began to rain the very day the order was obeyed and it continued until the rivers were full and flowing swiftly.

Elizabeth devoted Wednesdays to her village clinics and Edgar gave Thursdays to his. The country people loved them both—the bright-eyed, smiling, energetic little lady with her curly brown hair drawn to the top of her head; the tall, dark, quiet man who was so gentle and so skillful.

They went first to Bungamati, a village six miles south of Kathmandu, accessible only by jeep. They held clinic in a room that measured eight feet square by five and one half feet high.

"Edgar sits on the floor," wrote Elizabeth, "his back to the door, with his patient on the floor before him. The floor makes a surprisingly good and efficient examining table."

"First we spray the room to get rid of thousands of flies. Then we open our cases of instruments and medicines, pause for prayer, and begin to hold our clinic," Edgar added.

Later Edgar moved to a much larger and cleaner house in which he could stand erect. Then late in 1956 the men of Bungamati presented Edgar with a formal petition asking him to build a model clinic in the village. The petition carried 300 "signatures"—in the form of thumbprints—mute testimony to the lack of literacy in Nepal.

Deeply touched by this request, Edgar forwarded the petition to the Minister of Health and asked permission to proceed. Since foreigners may not buy land in Nepal and all proposed construction must be approved by the proper authorities, it was necessary to wait.

In due course, his request was approved. In 1957 Edgar and Elizabeth personally proposed to pay for the construction of a suitable dispensary as a memorial to their parents. However, they abandoned the idea when the headman of the village (a Buddhist whose niece was a nurse at Shanta Bhawan) offered to make a house available for the work rent-free. Edgar conducted regular clinics there as long as the Millers served in Nepal.

After going first to Bungamati with Edgar, Elizabeth started her own village clinic in Bonepa, a spot at least two hours by jeep from Kathmandu. With the help of two nurses she examined as many as 120 patients on each visit.

Early in 1958 she began going to Chapagaon with a team of helpers and continued to visit that area on Wednesdays until the spring of 1964. Then the work of all the doctors of the United Mission Hospital was reorganized and reassigned.

Chapagaon serves a more populous region than Bonepa or Bungamati and the number of patients ranged from 140 to 200. It lay only eight miles from Kathmandu, but what miles! The road was rutted, much of it uphill, and slippery in wet weather. On a good day it took the team an hour and fifteen minutes to reach the place in a jeep; on a bad day, an hour and three quarters. To brighten the journey as they started off they would sing lustily a bit of doggerel they had composed. This celebrated the terrible road, the diseases, the smells.

The first two times Elizabeth made the trip, she could not imagine why she felt the way she did when she got

41

home to Kathmandu. She took massive doses of aspirin in case she might be coming down with something. Then it dawned on her that her poor bones were objecting to jouncing up and down to and from Chapagaon. After that, she pretended she was a rag doll and lolled about during the ride as if she had no bones at all. When she remembered to do that, she had no more trouble.

Chapagaon, like every village in Nepal, had its large tank (pond) that the villagers used for washing themselves, their dishes, their clothes. Their animals took their baths in it, sometimes so many at once that the tank was suddenly a forest of horns. (In order to survive, buffaloes need a daily dunking.) The women beat their clothes on the rocks around it and washed their hair with the mud. (There must be something to this novel shampoo, Elizabeth thought. The women's hair is wonderfully thick and glossy.) Even the jars they used to draw drinking water from the village well were washed in the tank.

A long-range public health program to eliminate the causes of typhoid, diphtheria, smallpox, tuberculosis, cholera, tetanus, and poliomyelitis was a top priority. Elizabeth and her helpers pioneered; villagers were inoculated.

Week after week, year after year, they visited Chapagaon on Wednesdays, put in a twelve-hour day, cared for many ill patients and persevered in achieving a total immunization of the village. They succeeded. No epidemics have since been reported in Chapagaon.

Of course there were disappointments, failures, tragedies. Many people waited too long to come to the doctor. Others had incurable maladies. Ignorance took its toll. Abortions performed by people with no training resulted in many fatalities from lockjaw.

A typical day might go something like this:

From a village a father comes balancing two baskets on a shoulder pole, a sick baby in each basket. The doctor can treat them; they will recover their health.

There, however, goes a young mother, her baby in a basket on her back, her devoted husband following. The stout walking pole she carries is certain evidence that the family has traveled rugged paths to consult the doctor. Sad and without hope they retrace the three-day trek. The doctor says she can do nothing. The baby is hydrocephalic (abnormal amount of fluid in and enlargement of the skull, accompanied by brain damage). It is heartbreaking to explain and to receive such news. Even so the Nepalese say that this kind of experience gives them consolation; they are glad to know that the doctor tells the truth.

Now at the end of the day two friends bring in a very ill man on a litter. Why did he wait until everyone is tired, almost ready to close the clinic and go home? Because he has been on the way a long time over the mountain trails and has only just reached Chapagaon, hoping against hope that he wouldn't be too late to see the doctor. Anyone who lived in Chapagaon would have been waiting at the clinic long before the doctor arrived.

Sometimes it is not possible for friends or relatives to carry a patient all the way to Chapagaon. They take him to the road and stretch him out beside it, hoping that the doctor will stop on the way.

One Wednesday on the way to Chapagaon, Elizabeth was flagged down by a villager who was anxious about a 16-year-old Nepalese girl who expected her first baby and had been in labor for four days. To get to her Elizabeth had to stoop to enter the low doorway of the house, thread a path through a long passageway where buffaloes were stabled, climb a ladder in a far corner so dark she had to feel for the rungs to reach the second floor. There in a room approximately four feet square and four feet high, the girl lay writhing on a bed of straw.

Elizabeth immediately recognized that a distended bladder was obstructing the delivery, but since she had no sterile catheter with her, she went on to Chapagaon and sent back a trained Nepalese midwife with the necessary equipment.

Later the midwife returned with the good news that the emergency had been cared for and that the mother had a normal delivery.

How do they pay, these people who have so little?

If possible, they pay in money—otherwise in gifts. "Today," Edgar once wrote, "one patient brought four small lemons, one gave me six small oranges, another two eggs and the headman's son brought ten small bananas. Once in a while someone brings a live chicken. Occasionally the Buddhist priest presents a scarf, a highly significant gift. They are all so grateful."

What of the drain on the strength of the doctor and the helpers—the jolting journey, the pressure of sheer numbers, the battle against ignorance, the frustration of knowing that under different circumstances some could be healed who will not live?

As a Christian missionary doctor, Elizabeth tried to be as enthusiastic about the two-hundredth patient as she was about the first. To her, each was equally important and deserved her best.

Edgar commented more than once in his letters, "I have never seen Elizabeth work harder or go to bed more tired, but thank the Lord for sleep. We wake

45

up ready to go back to the work that we really love doing."

Edgar's clinical caseload was no less numerous, varied, frustrating, rewarding, absorbing and wearing. Frequently, many cases required more than one diagnosis because patients presented multiple symptoms. He had quantities of material and comments on diseases to add to the medical library given them by the Wilmington Academy of Medicine. His references to Elizabeth's hard work and weariness at the end of a day reflected his own activities and feelings; the letters they sent home were usually signed, "Elizabeth and Edgar," or "Edgar and Elizabeth."

CHAPTER FIVE
The United Mission Grows

The Nepalese measure distance in their country not by miles or kilometers but in days. What matters is the time it takes to walk from one place to another. Of what use is it to talk of distance as the crow flies when one's land is rugged and mountainous, when a trail may cross a ridge at 8,000 feet, plunge sharply 3,000 feet to cross a stream and then mount another ridge.

Within the first year of the existence of Shanta Bhawan Hospital, King Mahendra was on tour in his kingdom four days' walk from Kathmandu when he came upon a little girl with club feet. The King commanded the mother of the child to take her to Shanta Bhawan because he said that the doctors there could make her well. Not daring to disobey the King, the mother brought the child to the hospital and explained that the King had sent her.

47

Dr. Bethel Fleming manipulated the child's feet, stretched them and put them in a cast once a month. A year of this treatment proved successful; thereafter Bishnu, for that was her name, was able to run about in a normal manner. When she was discharged from the hospital her mother came to take her home. Not long afterward, the mother reappeared with Bishnu. She reported that the little girl was no longer content to stay in their village, that she wanted to live at the hospital.

"But the hospital is for people who are ill," they tried to explain.

After some discussion, it was agreed that they would find a job for the mother so that she could afford to stay in Kathmandu with Bishnu.

In spite of this arrangement, the mother soon disappeared, apparently abandoning Bishnu. The tender-hearted Millers had grown to love the child, so they decided to accept responsibility for her. They applied formally to the King to adopt her; the King consented.

A happy, sturdy child with expressive dark eyes, she was interested in everything that went on in Shanta Bhawan, helpful in her small way because of her fluency in Nepali and her increasing command of English.

One day Elizabeth surprised Bishnu, with a stethoscope, instructing a bed patient, an old lady, to roll nearer the edge of the bed so she could examine her.

Elizabeth told Edgar that the patient must have thought there was a dwarf M.D. on the staff, for she was complying with all Bishnu's instructions.

Catapulted into work in the clinic as soon as they arrived in the field, the Millers had been relying on interpreters and trying to study Nepali in the tag ends of time left from their many other duties. After they had been in Kathmandu for a year, it became possible to be released from duties in Shanta Bhawan so that they might concentrate on language study.

They went to India and spent two months in the spring of 1957 at Darjeeling. Of this experience Elizabeth wrote:

"Even though we are in the 'lisping, stammering' tongue stage of our Nepali language study, we feel that these two months have been most profitable. We can say a few things, but what is more important is that we can understand what is being said to us in a much easier fashion. One cannot be a very good doctor unless one is a good listener."

Upon their return to Kathmandu they continued to use interpreters much of the time to be sure they did not misunderstand what their patients said.

Elizabeth's interpreter afforded her much quiet amusement because of the unexpected twists she introduced into English. Elizabeth made notations of a few:

"Her stomach wants to baby." (She can't seem to get pregnant.)

"She is sore on the finger of her right leg (her toe) ."

"Fever is afraid of visiting her now." (It's gone.)

"Her one disease is much better. The other one is not good."

"Now is the time when she is quite worse."

"She has pain in both teeth."

The patients, for their part, would often take the interpreter to task, thinking she did not translate everything. Yet in spite of these difficulties, doctor and patient managed to communicate what was essential to the
job at hand.

The number of cooperating boards in the United
Mission as well as the number of missionaries continued
to increase steadily in these years; the fame of Shanta
Bhawan spread throughout Nepal.

Edgar made it a practice to inquire of his patients,
"How did you hear of Shanta Bhawan?" and he would
usually receive the reply, "Everyone in Nepal knows of
Shanta Bhawan."

In May, 1958, Robert Fleming reported that Shanta
Bhawan had established an all-time monthly high with
131 inpatients, 1006 outpatients.

In October an epidemic of cholera broke out. The
hospital staff was tested in a way that called for heroic
effort on the part of everyone. They offered their ser-

vices to the government director of health. He asked that they furnish intravenous solutions in large quantities and that they inaugurate a massive campaign of inoculations.

Immediately they began to prepare the precious intravenous fluid on a round-the-clock schedule and cast about for some way of obtaining enough bottles to contain it. They appealed to the hotels, which responded with all their empty whiskey bottles. "I never knew there were so many brands of whiskey," commented Edgar. Filled with intravenous solution, sterilized, and delivered to the cholera hospital—the same one which had originally shared its quarters with the United Medical Mission—every six bottles saved a life.

The sights in the cholera hospital appalled Edgar. Old and young, men and women and children lay stretched out on cots packed close together. They overflowed onto pallets on the floor or into tents. Out of every five, one died. A weeping and wailing family would carry the dying to the riverside to be cremated. When death was imminent, the dying patient was taken quickly to the river so that his feet could be dipped into the sacred water. If the river was reached before he died, his admission to heaven was assured. The Nepalese doctors worked long and faithfully.

At the same time teams of workers from Shanta

Bhawan, a doctor or a nurse with Nepalese health assistants, fanned out over the valley, visiting the villages and inoculating people wherever they might be found—on street corners, outside the temples, working in the fields. At first many people objected; inoculations were contrary to the will of their god who had decreed a certain number must die. However, when the headman of the village urged his people to accept the inoculations, they would do so. In some cases, villages sent requests for the teams to come. Before the epidemic was over, these teams had given about 8,000 injections.

A mild typhoid epidemic followed; the staff of Shanta Bhawan never forgot that year of 1958. However, they rejoiced at the news that the government had renewed their original contract for another ten years.

The year 1959 meant notable progress for Nepal, for the United Mission to Nepal, and for the Millers and the Flemings.

In February of that year, King Mahendra proclaimed a new constitution that preserved the absolute power of the king but established a democratic structure: two houses of parliament to be elected, a prime minister to be appointed by the king.

The headquarters of the United Mission moved from India to Nepal.

Through the generosity of the Salisbury, Maryland,

Methodist Church it became possible for the Flemings and the Millers to rent a two-story house near the hospital, which they always called the Salisbury bungalow. This afforded them a welcome degree of comfort and privacy not hitherto possible. They escaped from the noise of falling bed pans, of moaning patients, of constant coughing, the cries of babies and women in labor, and all the other noises that go with a hospital. Yet they were close enough to be on hand in emergencies.

The move enabled Shanta Bhawan to add thirty beds to its capacity.

During these first years, the United Mission also received permission to expand its program from medical work exclusively to include educational and agricultural work.

In January of 1958, Jonathan Lindell, who later became the United Mission's executive secretary, his wife and three daughters, Miss Rebecca Grimsrud of Wisconsin and Miss Nora Vickers of Yorkshire, England, left Kathmandu and trekked seventy-five miles to the west over the mountains to settle at a place called "The Pass of the Mango and Pipal Trees" and begin an educational and medical program. This was the first time Western women and children had attempted to live in this interior part of Nepal. As Mrs. Lindell reported in her first letter:

The wind is howling around the house tonight. All five of us are crowded into one small room which has only an opening for a door and no glass in the windows. Diet is confined to cereal, rice, unleavened bread and eggs. One day we had a gift of some meat, and another, spinach; no meat nor vegetables available to buy. In five minutes, Rachel (age one and a quarter) is dirty from head to foot. Yesterday the whole situation looked so hopeless. I can't do any settling for there's no place to settle. But I guess someone must have prayed for me because I crawled up to a little more on top of things today.

In the first three days, Miss Vickers saw fifty-six patients on the tiny veranda of her quarters and word spread rapidly through the mountains that medical help was available. So began this project.

Approximately one year later the Millers visited the Lindells and the nurses. They wanted to see the dispensary, the school, the agricultural programs. In order to do this, they went by plane to Pokhara and then trekked east through the mountains for four and one half days. They slept on air mattresses in pup tents. Elizabeth was so exhausted at the end of each day that she fell asleep on her air mattress as soon as it was inflated. The porters would erect the pup tent over her sleeping form and she would not wake again until she heard them taking the tent down in the morning.

They arrived at their destination late in the day, weary beyond all description, to find a crisis. That morning a young man with a hand in tatters from a gun explosion had come for help; Ampipal was not equipped to do the necessary surgery.

Hot tea laced with sugar revived the Millers. They set about preparing for an emergency operation. Fortunately, because the school construction program was under way, they found a carpenter's handsaw Edgar could use. The nurses at the dispensary produced the tiny bit of ether they had on hand. The women furnished needles and sutures. All of this equipment—handsaw, needles, sutures and the dressings—they boiled.

A low bench on the dirt floor served as the operating table, and all knelt around it, some to administer the ether, the others to hold flashlights.

"On our knees was a good place to be, considering all the circumstances," said Elizabeth.

Edgar's first attempt to amputate the hand did not produce a "good flap" as the surgeons call it, so he had to try again. This time all went well. The boy's arm healed perfectly without a sign of infection.

Some days later the Millers returned to Kathmandu, happy to have been of service, but glad to be back to everyday routine problems.

No one could measure the Christian influence of these doctors' work. Incidents, some major, some minor, encouraged them.

For instance, a boy was admitted so seriously ill with miliary tuberculosis that Elizabeth paused to consider whether it would be a waste to treat him with some of the precious small supply of medicine. However, she could not resist the appeal in his eyes, and administered it. Miraculously, the boy recovered and resolved to study medicine and become a doctor. Some day he hopes to be the head of Shanta Bhawan. He well might. Who is to say?

Another day a barefooted old man hobbled into Elizabeth's clinic. He had walked seven hours with a dislocated toe. Traction solved the problem, and the toe snapped back into place. While she applied a splint and a bandage to reinforce it until it healed, she noticed that he was weeping quietly.

"Am I hurting you?" she asked.

"No," he answered. "I was just so touched that you should be taking all this trouble over my dirty old toe."

Sometimes the battle with superstition and alien beliefs was lost; sometimes it was won.

"Today," wrote Edgar, "one patient complained of a bad toothache but she would not let me extract her tooth. Through an interpreter (she spoke Newari, not

Nepali) I learned that the day was not auspicious. She will permit me to pull it next week."

A prominent businessman with a serious heart ailment insisted on leaving the hospital to perform a religious rite in spite of Edgar's efforts to convince him that he would jeopardize his life, that he had a chance to recover if he would remain under treatment.

He returned to the hospital in such bad condition that Edgar knew he would die in a short time. A number of his friends gathered and asked to bring a cow into his room so that the cow could be taken to the priest for dedication to save the man's soul. "No," said Edgar. "We cannot allow such a thing."

The men persisted. Could they bring the cow to the door and extend a long rope from it to their friend for him to touch? Then his soul might still be saved.

"No," said Edgar. Then he explained, "We have a God we can talk to directly. If you will fold your hands and bow your heads, I will pray to him." Fifteen of the men bowed their heads reverently as Edgar prayed.

Travelers to Kathmandu visited Shanta Bhawan in increasing numbers as more and more tourists ventured to explore this hitherto unknown land. Some of them sought medical attention. Edgar remembers one of these, Francis Drake, an American, with particular gratitude.

Early in January, 1959, Mr. Drake came to the hospital at a time when Edgar was frantically busy with clinic patients. However, he stopped to examine Mr. Drake.

"There's not enough power today to take an electrocardiogram or an X-ray and that's what we need to do," explained Edgar. "Come back tomorrow."

Mr. Drake did just that. "What you need is a generator right here in the hospital," he remarked conversationally. "What would it cost?"

Preoccupied with the examination, Edgar didn't answer at first. Then he said, "Oh, offhand I'd say about three thousand dollars."

To Edgar's complete surprise, Mr. Drake reached for his prescription pad. "Okay," he said as he scrawled an I.O.U. for three thousand dollars on it. "If you find it costs more than that, let me know."

Edgar sent a young Mennonite volunteer to India to shop for a generator. When he returned, he reported that he had found a suitable one in Calcutta. It was a bargain, he said, for the dealer, a Hindu, had unaccountably cut the price by several hundred rupees when he explained why he wanted it. However, by the time they paid to transport it from Calcutta over the mountains, and constructed a building to house it, the total bill came to $3,800.

Edgar wrote to Mr. Drake and told him this, since he had suggested he do so. Before long the full amount arrived with a note from Mr. Drake saying that he secured half of the money from Laurance Rockefeller.

In April of 1960, Edgar reported these statistics for Shanta Bhawan:

Medical beds	50
Surgical	23
Maternity	7
Bassinets	7
Pediatrics	10

Total number of patients admitted to the hospital in 1959 1753

Number of outpatients in 1959 15,224

Major operations	306	
Minor operations	564	
Deliveries	133	(Of these 50 were abnormal)
Number of doctors	4,	one on furlough and one on a month's holiday, and a visiting surgeon for two weeks
Number of nurses	18	graduates
Nurses in training	12	
Laboratory technicians	3	

Number employed in skilled tasks and number of additional workers 20

In addition, they broke ground on April 14, 1960, for a new wing to the outpatient department.

It seemed impossible that all this had been accomplished in only four years.

CHAPTER SIX
Crosscurrents in Kathmandu

Kathmandu in those early years of the United Mission to Nepal seemed a particularly appropriate setting in which to carry out the words of the commissioning service, "Go into all the world and preach the gospel . . ." instead of the missionaries' going into the world, the world seemed to be coming into Kathmandu.

Names of visitors from twenty-seven different countries and from every continent studded the guest book that the Millers kept during the nine years they served as missionaries to Nepal. At various government functions that they attended, they met representatives of still other countries.

As missionaries, they had more freedom to meet and mingle with visitors from China and Russia than did their friends in the United States government agencies, for these were bound by political considerations.

For instance, when the government of Nepal received a delegation from Communist China headed by Premier Chou En-lai, Bethel Fleming and Elizabeth Miller accepted invitations to a reception in their honor. Elizabeth, an amateur photographer, took her movie camera and trained it on various distinguished guests. She devoted particular attention to one Chinese man resplendent in a bright red uniform, under the impression that she was photographing Chou En-lai. Later she and Bethel were introduced to the Premier. They noted that he was wearing a simple black tunic. Speaking perfect English, he invited them to visit China any time they wished. Who the man in the impressive uniform was they never discovered.

Queen Elizabeth and Prince Philip visited Kathmandu. They were approachable and made a favorable impression. Elizabeth snapped a picture of the royal couple shortly before they set out for the Terai, the famous jungle hunting area of Nepal. Nepal had only sixty elephants, so the king rented 180 more from India to accommodate the royal party in appropriate style.

A group of Russians also came to Kathmandu. In connection with their proposal to build a hospital there, they visited Shanta Bhawan and were taken on a tour of inspection. Afterward, the Millers invited them to share their hospitality. One may long ponder the comments they wrote in the guest book:

"Two mountains never meet, but two persons can always meet."

"We are very grateful for the opportunity to visit the hospital. During our visit we could feel great love of the personnel toward their work. We wish the personnel of the hospital much success in their noble cause."

Shortly before the Millers left on furlough in the spring of 1961, the Russians did indeed begin to build a hospital in Kathmandu—a sixty-bed hospital that they planned to staff with six doctors. The government of Nepal with the assistance of the United States Operations Mission, remodeled and enlarged its hospital to 250-bed capacity. Truly, Shanta Bhawan had helped to achieve better health care for the people of Nepal.

Events that were taking place in the outside world during these years affected the United Mission in varying degrees.

The Chinese Communist invasion of Tibet drove an estimated 9,000 Tibetan refugees into Nepal, fully a third of them to Kathmandu. Every day some of these required treatment at the hospital and clinic.

In November, 1960, the personnel of the United Mission were deeply concerned about an Indian Christian from the National Missionary Society, Prem Pradhan, in Tansen, West Nepal, who was accused of converting nine Hindu Nepalese to Christianity and thereafter baptizing them. These men were employed in building the United Mission hospital in Tansen. All were jailed to await trial. Finally, after a year, they were tried and found guilty. Prem Pradhan was sentenced to six years and placed in prison in Kathmandu. Conviction was based on the law of the land that prohibits conversion to another religion; it illustrates some of the factors in the religious situation.

At the same time small groups of Christians were conducting the conventional activities of congregations in worship and witness in a number of places. One such group, under the leadership of men from the Mar Thoma Church in South India, built the first Christian chapel in Kathmandu. A second group started another.

The sudden political upheaval of December 15, 1960, in Nepal surprised everyone. The King suspended the constitution, arrested the cabinet, banned political parties and dismissed parliament.

During this period, the name of Shanta Bhawan seemed as magical a password in Nepal as "Open sesame" had been for Ali Baba. All those bound for Shanta Bhawan were passed immediately through check points.

The Millers will always remember January 24, 1961,

as the day on which they went to Delhi to meet Edgar, Jr. (Tyke) and Jane who had arranged to come and help as volunteers at Shanta Bhawan for three months.

Tall and dark like his father, Edgar, Jr. had never considered any career other than medicine. In his boyhood, he enjoyed visiting with his mother's patients while they waited to see her. One day she discovered him selling lemonade to them. He had charmed the Millers' faithful cook into making it.

By 1961, he had finished his residency in Rochester, N.Y. Jane, a trained nurse before her marriage to him, had taken a refresher course so that she could assist him during their time in Nepal. They found the experience invaluable. Much of the time Edgar, Jr. was the only surgeon in Nepal. He did orthopedic and many other types of surgery. He performed the first lung surgery ever undertaken in Nepal, thus adding to the long list of "firsts" for the United Mission.

He and his father visited a tuberculosis sanitarium six miles from Kathmandu and selected cases to bring to Shanta Bhawan for surgery. At first, he would operate from early morning until ten o'clock at night in an attempt to keep up with the number of surgery cases his father brought to him. Then one day he said, "Gee, Dad. Let's call a halt for a bit. I can't maintain this pace."

He and Jane hardly had time to be homesick for their three children in the United States.

The Nepalese loved this attractive young couple. They received from them the same compassion shown by the senior Millers. Edgar, Jr. returned their regard. His concern for his patients took precedence over his enjoyment of such pleasures as the tiger hunt to which the second prince had invited him and Jane. They went for two days, but then even though protocol would have allowed him to shoot on the third day, he chose to fly to Kathmandu to see several of his post-operative patients.

All the Millers enjoyed these three months—the pleasure of being together once more, sharing their love of the Nepalese, their interest in the different ways of doing things, the beauty of Nepal.

On April 15, they left Kathmandu together. The senior Millers began their furlough to the United States by way of Calcutta, Bangkok, Hong Kong, Tokyo and Honolulu, arriving in San Francisco on May 3. They enrolled Bishnu in a boarding school in Kalimpong, India, for the time when they would be away.

Furlough brought a welcome reunion with family and with many friends. It also brought a schedule of speechmaking that covered fourteen states, including Florida and California.

"Speaking is not our specialty; it was not easy," wrote Edgar, "but we both felt blessed beyond description. We have been so inspired, uplifted and encouraged. We are determined that with God's help we will be better missionaries. . . .

"We find that our people here at home are hungry, interested and spiritually alive as they seem so eager to listen, to learn and to help."

During this year of the Millers' furlough, the United Mission received permission from the government of Nepal to open medical, educational and agricultural work in the region south of Mt. Everest and in the far and isolated west. Robert Fleming reported this; he appealed for more missionaries:

"Our experience has proved that local personnel find it extremely difficult to initiate new work, but they fit in quickly once the program is under way. We need Western workers to pioneer in these new fields. Don't you know of some young, well-qualified medico, nurse, teacher or farmer who would like to join the United Mission to Nepal and work with the high Himalayas as his horizon?"

Also, during this year, the United Mission acquired a second Kathmandu palace named Surendra Bhawan which made it possible to enlarge Shanta Bhawan to 120 beds. The first class of five student nurses was graduated from Shanta Bhawan, took the Florence Nightingale pledge, and lit candles as a token of their commitment!

CHAPTER SEVEN
Heartbreak and Hope

Before their return to the field for a second term, the Millers spent six weeks in Kalimpong, India, in language study. Then they plunged again into the ever-expanding programs of Shanta Bhawan Hospital. Elizabeth continued her weekly visits to the clinic at Chapagaon and Edgar to his work in the clinic at Bunganati, in addition to their regular schedules in Kathmandu.

Thursdays were leprosy clinic days at Shanta Bhawan. Soon after the hospital was first opened, the Millers and the Flemings realized that they needed to add leprosy to their list of priorities because so many of the Nepalese were its victims. They saw patients with it daily in their clinics and estimated that a growing percentage of the people suffered from it; three to four thousand of them lived in the valley of Kathmandu.

The doctors were determined to find, arrest and cure as many cases as they could.

Back in 1956, they had been visited by a representative of the Leprosy Mission of London, which operated twenty-four leprosy hospitals in India, others elsewhere. The staff hoped that this organization might become one of the cooperating groups in the United Mission to Nepal and thereafter send one of its qualified doctors to direct its efforts.

Two years later the Leprosy Mission joined as an associate member and assigned Dr. P. Chandy, a Christian from South India with a lifetime of experience in treating leprosy, as its Kathmandu representative.

Elizabeth took particular interest in these cases although she had never seen a person suffering from leprosy before coming to Nepal. One of the earliest cases she diagnosed as leprosy, a diagnosis in which Dr. Chandy concurred, involved a woman patient who had a large ulcer on her foot. Questioning revealed that a rat had chewed her foot while she slept. The patient hadn't felt the rat bites because in leprosy there is often a loss of sensation in hands and/or feet.

People came to the clinics not as untouchables but as any other patients. Dr. Pedley, also of the Leprosy Mission, and the United Mission nurse, Miss Meisel of Berlin, helped to handle the crowds at Shanta Bhawan.

All of the staff felt with Dr. Chandy that it was most important to build up self-respect in individuals cut off by taboos, so that they might be reclaimed and reinstated in society. One leprosy patient, a young man in his early twenties, used to shake hands with Dr. Robert Fleming every time he saw him. Dr. Fleming noted the improvement in the man and his attitude.

CHAPTER EIGHT
A Crown of Life

Once again the Millers' guest book received names of visitors from many nations who enjoyed their hospitality. They entertained the American Everest expedition, mission tour groups, Ford Foundation experts, members of the United States Agency for International Development, embassy personnel, Nepalese government officials, doctors, nurses, public health workers from all over the world, personnel of many of the mission boards.

Of the round of their activities, Elizabeth once commented, "We hop from the heights to the depths; we go from the sublime to the ridiculous; we have the pleasure of associating with kings and queens and of befriending the poverty stricken; we have our joys and sorrows; but above all, we have the glorious assurance of your prayers and your love and that our Father God holds the world in his hands."

Many changes were taking place in Nepal in these years. On April 19, 1963, King Mahendra inaugurated a new type of government for Nepal, the Panchayat system. This called for a representative grouping of a different sort from the parliament he had dissolved in 1960.

Economic changes were transforming the nation. The Trisuli hydroelectric project gave great promise. An expanded system of air transport was making Kathmandu more accessible. Improvements in communication were taking place.

In 1963, the Leprosy Mission began the construction of the first building of a colony, the Anandaban Leprosy Hospital, on a lovely, pine-covered hillside on the rim of the capital valley about ten miles from Kathmandu. Dr. Chandy was named superintendent.

During one of Dr. Chandy's annual vacations, Elizabeth acted as the doctor in charge. In May, 1963, Edgar wrote from Anandaban, "There are seventy leprosy patients here and eventually there will be 250. Only the worst cases are admitted; for example, those who have huge ulcers on their feet or those who have no feet at all. There are a number of children. One of them has a foot drop. Several are without noses; some show the typical claw hands and big nodules. Many are without several of their digits, their fingers or their toes.

"It is amazing how happy the patients seem to be. They sing. Many work hard, making small gardens or building stone walls to hold this mountainside together. How they love to tend flower or vegetable gardens. Some become severely ill because of their disease, but modern methods of treatment can make even the sickest comfortable. What wonderful care these patients receive! No wonder they feel so much more secure where they are not isolated.

"Little did I think when I read about cases of leprosy in the Bible that we would ever be living in a leprosy colony where Elizabeth would set a schedule for herself to examine thoroughly at least seven patients a day in addition to making general rounds."

At that time the work of building the hospital was in progress. By late 1963 it was ready for dedication. The staff invited King Mahendra to cut the ribbon. He did so in April, 1964, an act that symbolized his endorsement of the work of the Leprosy Mission and the United Mission.

During his visit, the King made rounds of all the wards. He also wanted to see for himself the unique "hydram" pump which used a downward flow of water from another direction to force water up three hundred feet into the hospital tanks. "So down over the mountainside we went," wrote Edgar, "in His Majesty's jeep with the King, the Queen and the Princess. We then carefully walked down the stony path to the pump station. What a King! He is interested in everything."

The United Mission, nearing its tenth anniversary, reported a missionary force of 102 persons, twenty-five participating boards, ten projects.

The Church of Christ of Nepal, an indigenous body, claimed congregations totalling 300 persons in about twenty places.

Meanwhile, on October 27, 1963, at 3:40 P.M. precisely, King Mahendra honored Edgar by conferring a royal decoration and a title upon him in recognition of his services as physician to the royal family of Nepal.

An increasing number of younger doctors came to serve in the medical mission program. The Millers were reassured, for they reluctantly recognized that they could not maintain the strenuous schedule they had adopted, without increasing fatigue. Edgar suffered a troublesome illness that affected his hearing.

One day when he was summoned to the royal palace to attend the Queen Mother, he realized that he could not hear her heartbeat and had to depend on palpating her wrist.

Then as Edgar was conducting the outpatient clinic at Shanta Bhawan one day, a visitor entered and introduced himself as a specialist in neurology.

"Good," said Edgar. "I have two or three cases I'd like to consult you about."

"No," said the doctor gently, "I have come to examine you."

When he had completed his examination, he said, "I'm sorry to have to tell you this, but in the interest of your own health, you should go back to the United States as soon as it can be arranged."

So it was that the Millers regretfully prepared to leave Nepal.

One of Edgar's last acts was to give a written request to King Mahendra to release Prem Pradhan from prison. On His Majesty's birthday, June 11, 1965, the pastor was granted a reduced sentence and released along with 300 other prisoners, several weeks after the Millers had left Kathmandu.

In their farewell letter from Nepal, Edgar wrote:

"After nine years we both ask, 'Who do these Nepalese say that we are?' We are more concerned over their interpretation of our ministry here than with whether we have been effective doctors. They are a wonderful, spirited people and sent many letters and gestures of gratitude to all of us at the hospital for the attention, the loving care, and all paramedical help. It has been a privilege to attend and mingle with these people.

"I must say that these latter years have been the most

rewarding, exciting and challenging. There have been more tears of sorrow and joy, more frustrations and victories, more disappointments and exaltations than could have happened to us in the homeland.

"But who do people say that we are? I do know Elizabeth has been an ideal missionary. She has given of herself. I have been inspired by her ability to win a smile from the poorest to the richest. We will both miss the drama and romance of this rapidly changing practice. Our only regret is that we are not forty years younger."

* * *

Prominently displayed in the Millers' guest house at their retirement home in Liverpool, Pennsylvania, is a framed relief map of Nepal which measures perhaps twelve by eighteen inches. Of thin hammered silver, with the place names delicately painted in red in graceful Hindi characters, the map shows the jagged peaks of the Himalayas in faithful detail. A tiny blue-bordered red pennant—the official swallowtail flag of Nepal —marks Mount Everest on the roof of the world.

Elizabeth treasures this map more than anything she and Edgar brought home. Part of her sentiment is due to her appreciation of the fine workmanship, but chiefly it is because Dr. Malla gave it to them.

Before Nepal was open to the West, or international

and American assistance programs ever began, or any transportation was available, Dr. Malla walked out of Nepal to study medicine in India. He followed this by taking advanced work in public health in the United States—the first Nepalese to come here for study. Then he returned to Nepal to try to apply what he had learned.

He had a great deal to do with persuading the government to invite the Flemings to open the medical mission. Now one of his daughters and two of his sons are medical doctors.

To Elizabeth, Dr. Malla was the real pioneer of medical work in Nepal.

CHAPTER NINE
Once More Unto the Breach

"After we are rested there may be other vineyards that will need laborers," Edgar wrote six months after he and Elizabeth settled down in Pennsylvania, ostensibly to retire. "We hope not so far away—but with real challenge. In the meantime, we are taking refresher courses in our own specialties. God hasn't revealed our future field, but by faith I know he will lead us as he has in the past." Shortly after this, they learned that the Albert Schweitzer Hospital in Deschapelles, Haiti, needed volunteers.

In 1956, while the Millers sailed for India and Nepal on the *Steel Surveyor,* the hospital in Haiti admitted its first patients. Its administrator, Dr. Larry Mellon, spent almost as many years on the road to the place where he wanted to be as the Millers had.

A grandnephew of multimillionaire Andrew W. Mellon, William Larimer Mellon, Jr. dropped out of Princeton after completing his freshman year. He failed to find any satisfaction in the family banking business, even less as a salesman in the family oil business. He turned his back on the business world forever and bought two ranches in Arizona. He took to the rough outdoor life of a ranch hand and learned the rugged tasks of a cowboy. His ranches prospered.

After a tour of duty with the Office of Strategic Services in Europe during World War II, he returned to Arizona and married.

However, life on the ranch wasn't enough. Restless, he chanced upon a *Life* magazine article about Dr. Albert Schweitzer and his devotion to the Lambaréné Hospital in Gabon, Africa. Larry Mellon read it with quickening interest, then delved deeper into the life, work and philosophy of Dr. Schweitzer to the point where he thought of little else.

He decided to become a doctor and, like Dr. Schweitzer, to go where medical service was non-existent. Encouraged by his wife, he enrolled at Tulane University to finish his college work and then to study medicine— a program that required seven years to complete. When he made this decision, he was thirty-eight years old. His wife studied with him, taking courses that would equip her to become a medical technician.

When Dr. Schweitzer visited the United States in 1949, Larry arranged to meet and talk with him; in 1951, while in Africa, Larry and his wife spent some time at Lambaréné.

They spent the following year on a research assignment in rural Haiti, and decided that this was the place of greatest need, that they really belonged in Deschapelles.

By agreement with the Haitian government, they undertook to build, equip and operate a modern hospital, using their own funds. In return, they would receive a rent-free location, free water rights, and land enough to operate a farm that would supply fresh produce for the hospital. Haiti would allow medicines and supplies to come to the hospital duty free. Though the administration changed between the time this contract was signed and the time the Mellons opened their hospital, every part of it was honored by the succeeding regime.

In 1953, while Larry continued his course at Tulane, Mrs. Mellon lived in Haiti so that she could oversee the construction of the hospital. It was dedicated in 1954 and opened in 1956.

Deschapelles is in Haiti's Artibonite Valley where the completion of a government dam is causing a population boom. Previously the area had no doctors, only a small government maternity unit. Its undernourished people subsisted in grinding poverty, practiced voodoo, and died young with tuberculosis, malaria, yaws and intestinal parasites. In the beginning they were fearful about trusting the foreign doctors, but their fears proved groundless. During the hospital's first year and a half, 13,000 patients were treated.

Though Dr. Mellon poured most of his personal fortune into the enterprise, the constantly expanding program raised costs each year. Now it is necessary to solicit financial support and gifts of supplies and equipment from service groups, public-spirited corporations and the public.

Dr. Mellon has always hoped that increasingly Haitians would become qualified to serve on the staff and eventually run their own hospital, but as yet this dream has not come true. Meanwhile, the enormity of the challenge has drawn doctors, nurses and other professionally qualified people of varying religious beliefs and backgrounds from everywhere.

The Millers wrote to offer their services for three months—"stretching our medical wings a bit to see if they would still work"—was the way Elizabeth expressed it. Back came a prompt and favorable response.

Once again they packed their belongings, left their comfortable cottage amid the trees in Liverpool, Pennsylvania, and set off to help people in need of medical attention. They began their service the first of January, 1967.

Once again they found themselves carrying full working schedules in a hospital jammed to the doors each day with suffering humanity. Clinic began at 7:30 A.M. and continued until eight or nine at night. After that it usually took another hour to scan reports and check X-rays. Once again they undertook to learn another language—the Creole of the rural Haitians.

They found the climate as bad as Calcutta's; the heat and humidity were such that they perspired all day even though the nights were frequently cool enough to require a blanket.

Each morning after all the patients were registered in the clinic, their charts were assigned to the appropriate staff person—surgeon, pediatrician, midwife, or general practitioner—forty to each, usually.

Then the sick moved through the clinic in a never-ending stream. The Millers found here all the old familiar diseases they had come to know so well in Nepal: tuberculosis, intestinal parasites, malnutrition (much worse than it was in Nepal), leprosy (not so prevalent), typhoid, tetanus, and terrible anemias.

One of the cases which stands out in everyone's mind is that of a boy with pericarditis (fluid around the heart). Edgar, taking his courage in his hands, tapped the boy's heart four times and drained out the excess fluid. The two staff doctors were glad to have an opportunity to observe this technique, for it had not been used at the Schweitzer Hospital before.

Edgar treated many patients with decompensated hearts by giving massive doses of digitalis intravenously. Sometimes this resulted in a dramatic recovery. He taught this technique to Elizabeth.

"The Mellons have made this hospital a reality in a land that looks like a dusty, faded stage set," Elizabeth wrote, "and it draws all people to it."

In the entire three months the Millers took only two weekends off—one of these when Tyke and Jane flew over from Florida to surprise them.

Toward the end of their stay they became so tired that Edgar's ear trouble flared up again. More than one morning Elizabeth awoke to find that she had fallen asleep fully clothed the night before. In spite of all this, they found it difficult to pull up stakes and leave.

"Our steps are dragging and our heart strings are being pulled," Elizabeth wrote. "We just don't want to leave this dear place. How is it that these experiences so get under one's skin?"

They came home to their cottage in April. Bishn

was on Easter vacation from school. Spring was coaxing the tulips to bloom in their garden and the orioles warbled joyously from the tops of their tall trees. Swallows were building a nest in their garage. Retirement seemed somewhat more acceptable than before. There were still many ways to serve.

In September, a mission hospital in Port de Paix, Haiti, asked Elizabeth to come there for a month's assignment. Hurricanes had already started their yearly rampage through the Caribbean. Elizabeth didn't stop to consider them. She collected a few essentials, returned to Haiti, and took her place on the mission hospital staff.

One day she went to a distant village to hold clinic. With her in the station wagon was a class of student nurses to help the experienced nurses give shots, a general handyman in case they needed to change a tire, one boy who was a hospital helper, and Caroline Bradshaw, the missionary in charge at Port de Paix—some 16 or 17 passengers in all. That day they gave 1,000 children typhoid, DPT (diphtheria, whooping cough and tetanus) or BCG (tuberculosis) shots.

While they were doing this, a young man brought in his pregnant wife and asked that she be taken to the hospital to have her baby. Elizabeth wasn't afraid of complications and therefore considered such a trip un-

85

necessary, but the husband insisted. It would be their first child and he wanted to be sure nothing went wrong. Accordingly, one boy rode on the hood to make room and the party rearranged themselves so that the wife could lie on the floor as they prepared to return to Port de Paix.

None of them had eaten lunch and the wife seemed quiet, so about 3:30 in the afternoon they turned aside to picnic in a grove of almond trees near the sea. No sooner had they done this than Elizabeth realized that the woman had gone into labor and that the baby might arrive any minute. Not expecting to be confronted with a delivery, the team of workers had no proper equipment and had to improvise in a hurry.

Fortunately, one of the boys knew people who lived nearby; he went to them for a fresh palm mat. Elizabeth used the leftover alcohol sponges from the shots to sterilize a pair of scissors as well as a razor belonging to one of the boys and cleansed her hands with pre-moist disposable towelettes. Delivery was normal and a baby boy arrived in short order.

His mother wanted to name him after Elizabeth, but she refused to allow this.

"What is your husband's name?" asked the mother.

That's how the newborn Edgar Miller the 4th received his name.

Elizabeth waded into the sea to wash her hands, and once more the station wagon set out for Port de Paix.

*　*　*　*

Today, the Millers feel more deeply convinced than ever of the truth of something Elizabeth wrote from language school in Darjeeling years before, "People are the same everywhere. Their mode of dress is truly dissimilar. Their customs, and even their color varies, but at heart we are all alike. God holds the world in his hands."

*R*ECOGNITION

Citation to the Drs. Miller from Dickinson College, Carlisle, Pa.:

DICKINSON COLLEGE

Citation for distinguished public service

Edgar R. Miller   and   Elizabeth Bucke Miller
Class of 1920   Class of 1923

October 8, 1966 Founders Day Convention

Each of you and both of you together underscore the qualities Dickinson holds most dear. Using your talents and training in the medical profession, for twenty-eight years you (Dr. Edgar) served as cardiac specialist and you (Dr. Elizabeth) as internist in the city of Wilmington, Delaware. There you found friends and comfort, raised a family, and enjoyed satisfaction in the preservation of life.

For most people such an investment of self in the needs

of others is reward enough, but ten years ago you heard a distant, more demanding call from the valleys of the Himalayas. This was a call not merely to service but heroic service. For nine years you served together in the United Mission Hospital in Kathmandu (Nepal). Here you became symbols of Christian succor and of the practical conservation of lives which, without you, would have had little hope.

To you both, who would disclaim any mention of sacrifice, for your service—domestic, world-wide, and spiritual—we give you not only our thanks but our appreciation for suggesting to us how more Dickinsonians may seek to serve man and God.

(signed) Samuel W. Witwer, Jr.   Howard L. Rubendall
President Board of Trustees   President of the College

———◆•◆———

Citation to Elizabeth Bucke Miller beautifully hand lettered in black, red and gold:

The Alumnae Association of
The Woman's Medical College of Pennsylvania
confers this
Achievement Award
on
Elizabeth Bucke Miller, M.D.
Class of 1927
In recognition of her many years in the practice of medi-

cine, and especially for her work in bringing medical services to the people of Nepal.

By her outstanding work as a medical missionary she has set an example of selflessness by giving of herself to help others in need. In doing so she has served her profession with distinction and has brought honor to her Alma Mater and to women in medicine.

Given in Philadelphia	Doris G. Bartuska, M.D.
June 6, 1966	President, Alumnae Association

⋙◆◆⋘

Statement accompanying decoration conferred upon Dr. Edgar Miller by the King of Nepal, October 27, 1963 at 3:40 P.M.

Shree Dr. Edgar R. Miller being a worthy, is entitled to wear this title "Gorkha Dakstshiva Bahu" and is authorized to have respect and privilege related to this title given.

By the order of His Majesty
Nepal

The title means, "right hand of the Gorkhas" or "right hand of the royal family."

And Finally . . .

President Johnson added a postscript to the Millers' association with the royal family of Nepal. In 1967, when King Mahendra and Queen Ratna visited the

90

United States, Elizabeth and Edgar were among the guests at a state dinner held at the White House in honor of the royal couple. The next night Bishnu was with them at King Mahendra's reception honoring President Johnson.

READING LIST
Other Biographies

Bainton, Roland H. *Here I Stand: A Life of Martin Luther*. Nashville: Abingdon Press, 1950.

Carlson, Lois. *Monganga Paul* (The Congo ministry and martyrdom of Paul Carlson, M.D.). New York: Harper and Row, Publishers, Inc., 1966.

Crawford, Isabel. *Joyful Journey* (autobiography). Philadelphia: The Judson Press, 1951.

Davey, Cyril J. *Kagawa of Japan*. Nashville: Abingdon Press, 1961.

Gallagher, Teresa. *Give Joy to My Youth,* a Memoir of Dr. Tom Dooley, 1927-1961. New York: Farrar, Straus and Giroux, 1965.

Graham, Billy. *World Aflame*. Garden City: Doubleday & Co., Inc., 1965.

Harrison, Ann M. *A Tool in His Hand* (Dr. Paul W. Harrison, medical missionary in Arabia). New York: Friendship Press, 1958.

Harkness, Georgia. *John Calvin*. Nashville: Abingdon Press, 1958.

Holt, Rackham. *George Washington Carver:* An American Biography. Garden City: Doubleday & Co., Inc., 1942.

Homan, Helen Walker. *Francis and Clare,* Saints of Assisi. New York: Farrar, Straus and Giroux, 1956.

Kaunda, Kenneth. *A Humanist in Africa.* (Letters to Colin Morris from Kenneth Kaunda, President of Zambia). Nashville: Abingdon Press, 1967.

Lacy, Creighton. *Frank Mason North* (Social and Ecumenical Leader). Nashville: Abingdon Press, 1967.

Lash, Joseph P. *Dag Hammarskjöld*. Garden City: Doubleday and Co., Inc., 1961.

Lazell, J. Arthur. *Alaskan Apostle* (The Life Story of Sheldon Jackson). New York: Harper and Row, Publishers, Inc., 1960.

Mathews, Basil. *Livingstone the Pathfinder*. New York: Friendship Press, 1954.

Means, Florence Crannell. *Sagebrush Surgeon* (Dr. Clarence Salsbury, surgeon in the Navaho country). New York: Friendship Press, 1956.

Monk, Robert C. *John Wesley*. Nashville: Abingdon Press, 1966.

Nolan, Liam. *Small Man of Nanataki* (Kiyoshi Watanabe). New York: E. P. Dutton, and Co., 1966.

Oliver, Robert T. *Syngman Rhee,* The Man Behind the Myth. New York: Dodd, Mead and Co., 1964.

Perkins, Sara. *Red China Prisoner* (autobiography). Westwood, N.J.: Fleming H. Revell Co., 1963.

Petersen, William J. *Another Hand on Mine* (The Story of Dr. Carl K. Becker of Africa Inland Mission). New York: McGraw-Hill Book Co., Inc., 1967.

Prichard, Marianna Nugent and Norman Young Prichard. *Ten Against the Storm* (Biographies of ten courageous Japanese Christian leaders). New York: Friendship Press, 1957.

Rowland, Stanley J., Jr. *Men for Others* (Short biographies). New York: Friendship Press, 1965.

Rudolph L. C. *Francis Asbury*. Nashville: Abingdon Press, 1966.

Seamands, John T. *Pioneers of the Younger Churches.* Nashville, Abingdon Press, 1967.

Searcher, Victor. *Farewell to Lincoln.* Nashville: Abingdon Press, 1965.

Stuart, John Leighton. *Fifty Years in China* (The Memoirs of John Leighton Stuart, missionary and ambassador). New York: Random House, 1954.

Wilson, Dorothy Clarke. *Dr. Ida,* The Story of Dr. Ida Scudder of Vellore. New York: McGraw-Hill Book Co., Inc., 1959.

Wilson, Dorothy Clarke. *Handicap Race.* New York: McGraw-Hill Book Co., Inc., 1967. (A paraplegic ministers to other handicapped persons.)

Wilson, Dorothy Clarke. *Take My Hands:* The Story of Dr. Mary Verghese. New York: McGraw-Hill Book Co., Inc., 1963.

Wilson, Dorothy Clarke. *Ten Fingers for God* (Dr. Paul W. Brand, Vellore). New York: McGraw-Hill Book Co., Inc., 1965.

N.B. If some of these books are not available in bookstores, perhaps they may be borrowed from neighborhood libraries.